Welcome Basket Series

FAITH

(Core Principles of Our Journey)

Published By Carissa Brown

A Note for Carissa B.

God is so amazing. I bring this book back to our Father. Thank you, Lord, for allowing me to write the words on paper for your people. We dedicate this book back to you.
Thank you to my husband and everyone who has supported me.

FAITH (CORE OF OUR JOURNEY)
Table of Contents

FAITH (CORE OF OUR JOURNEY)

Faith is one of those foundational principles, and it's active, so we accepted our journey with Christ. We activate our spiritual belief system after we have had the encounter with the acceptance of Christ. When you receive the scripture content in John 3:16 and Romans 10:9-10 in your personal life, you are on a new journey. Many of us have had different encounters in our one-on-one moments with Jesus. This activation alone brings unlimited encounters of Faith-refill as you go through life.

Level after level, walking through each assignment, you are building yourself in the most Holy of Holies. So, let us dive into the welcome basket. Faith is belief, loyalty, and trust in God. The thing that stuck out the most is the trust in God. Let me be honest with you; when you finish this book, I believe you will comprehend the words "complete trust" in our Lord.

In the New Testament, John 10:7-11, Jesus talks about himself being the Good Shepherd,

"Then Jesus said to them again, "Most assuredly, I say to you, I am the door of the sheep. 8 All who ever came before Me are thieves and robbers, but the sheep did not hear them. 9 I am the door. If anyone enters by Me, he will be saved and

will go in and out and find pasture. 10 The thief does not come except to steal, kill, and destroy. I have come that they may have life, and that they may have it more abundantly.11 "I am the good shepherd. The good shepherd gives His life for the sheep." NKJV

The Lord came into this world to bring the prophecy to pass. Jesus Christ is our Savior. He taught the disciples and everyone he could reach that he had knocked on the door of our hearts, and if we let him in, we would have an abundant life. Jesus came into the world to save our lives, his assurance of us receiving him was not wavering, nor did he question why and what he said. Like Father, like Son, we can go back to the beginning of time (John 1:1-4).

"In the beginning was the Word, and the Word was with God, and the Word was God. 2 He was in the beginning with God. 3 All things were made through Him, and without Him, "Then Jesus said to them again, "Most assuredly, I say to you, I am the door of the sheep. 8 All who ever came [a]before Me are thieves and robbers, but the sheep did not hear them. 9 I am the door. If anyone enters by Me, he will be saved and will go in and out and find pasture. 10 The thief does not come except to steal, and to kill, and to destroy. I have come that they may have life, and that they may have it more abundantly.11 "I am the good shepherd. The good shepherd gives His life for the sheep." Nothing was made that was made. 4 In Him was life, and the life was the light of men."KJV

We can trace faith as a core principle from the beginning of time. Our God created the Heavens and the Earth. Genesis 1:1-

29. Then it begins. There were some incredible encounters at various levels of faith throughout the Old Testament.

Introduction

In recent years, I found myself in a season where I discovered it was vigorous to navigate certain parts of my life. The things that were uncomplicated for me became considerably harder; new obstacles were added to my life, which was already full of drawbacks. Doubt ran across my mind; I was searching for answers that were perplexing and I anticipating being answered.

At the beginning of this book, I mentioned "free fall faith." Yes, that did not exist anymore. I found myself reluctant to do anything unless there were truly divine signs. How do you convey that you were a faith walker, and now your Faith was bonded by

what seems to be bondage? Where did it come from? Why was it so hard? When did I get here?

Level after level, walking through each assignment, you are building yourself in the most Holy of Holies. So, let us dive into the welcome basket. Faith is belief, loyalty, and trust in God. The thing that stuck out the most is the trust in God. Let me be honest with you, by the time you finish this book, I believe you will comprehend the words "complete trust" in our Lord.

Genesis 12:1-3

Now the LORD had said unto Abram, Get thee out of thy country, and from thy kindred, and from thy father's house, unto a land that I will shew thee:² And I will make of thee a great nation, and I will bless thee, and make thy name great; and thou shalt be a blessing:³ And I will bless them that bless thee, and curse him that curseth thee: and in thee shall all families of the earth be blessed. KJV

As time went on, his Faith was challenged in many ways. He would receive a new name and more. Every encounter brings God glory all the time.

The first verse of Genesis 22 is powerful and prophetic, and we should be inclined to do this when we hear the voice of the Lord. Abraham was in a place of fulfillment at this time. You know he had his son and lived his life through different trials and tribulations.

Abraham is known to be the father of many nations, and in this chapter, he did not even know it. He was about to get an assignment that would change the lives of generations to come. His biggest test was about to come. One day, the Lord called upon him, and he responded," Here I am."

Reflection Time:

In the modern day, could you honestly respond as Abraham responded, or would you second guess if that were the Lord speaking to you at all?

According to the Word, Abraham responded with obedience and went to where he would have to sacrifice his son. Further in the scriptures, Abraham and his son are preparing the sacrifice, and his son is aware that there are no sheep and questions Abraham about what they will sacrifice.

_____

_____

_____

_____

_____

_____

_____

_____

_____

My Response

I would be praying that the Lord would speak, but there was silence. Abraham was in an act of response and tied up his son. He put his son on the altar and prepared to sacrifice him. God called his name, and once again, he replied, "Here I Am." Due to the obedience Abraham displayed, the Lord provided him with a ram to sacrifice and respond:

"Because you have obeyed me and have not withheld even your son, your only son, I swear by my own name that 17 I will certainly bless you. I will multiply your descendants beyond number, like the stars in the sky and the sand on the seashore. Your descendants will conquer the cities of their enemies. 18 And through your descendants all the nations of the earth will be blessed—all because you have obeyed me." NLT

The outcome was greater. Abraham is a notable example of Faith.

Reference Scriptures

Isaiah 40:31

[31] *But they that wait upon the LORD shall renew their strength; they shall mount up with wings as eagles; they shall run, and not be weary; and they shall walk, and not faint. KJV*

Romans 8:28

And we know that all things work together for good to them that love God, to them who are the called according to his purpose. KJV

James 2:18

But someone will say, "You have faith, and I have works." Show me your faith apart from your works, and I will show you my faith by my works. NLT

John 20:29

Jesus said to him, "Have you believed because you have seen me? Blessed are those who have not seen and yet have believed." KJV

2 Corinthians 5:6-7

So we are always of good courage. We know that while we are at home in the body we are away from the Lord, [7] for we walk by faith, not by sight. NKJV

Luke 17:6

And the Lord said, "If you had faith like a grain of mustard seed, you could say to this mulberry tree, 'Be uprooted and planted in the sea,' and it would obey you. KJV

Chapter 2: (Tunnel Faith)

Tunnel Faith takes place where you can experience faith engagement from different angles. When you are overwhelmed with the various angles, Tunnel Faith is a strategic approach, but you remind yourself that there is only one way: truly trust God through this strategic approach. I have experienced this approach and felt that this perception was valid. Spiritual Blinders or Blinkers is the tool in using this approach.

To understand the tunnel Faith approach, let us go to the Kentucky Derby; I have never personally attended one, but have seen them on TV and social media. One thing I noticed right off the top was the horse's face gear. The horse's face gear was covered with such manners. The horse's face gear is called

blinders or blinkers. Blinders are used to keep the horse's peripheral vision so that they cannot be distracted. With all the surrounding noises in their pit lanes, the blinders keep them visually focused when they take off in the race. Here, we can relate the gear to our strategic approach when there are many outside distractions. We must put on our spiritual blinders.

For some reason, this season, I experienced many angles of engaging in my Faith. I also activated another realm of faith and honestly did not know I had access to it. I had to go to the Bible's scriptures about the experience David (King David soon) had when Saul was after him. David hid in the cave and wilderness, waiting for God to tell him the next move. I am sure David was highly uncomfortable about not knowing the next move, but his whole confidence was in knowing God was with him. His "spiritual blinders" were geared toward him, and whatever came his way was not distracting. His obedience and use of his "spiritual blinders" gave him a strategic advantage whenever he encountered King Saul.

Some of you wonder when things will change or when it will be time to leave the cave. David was in the cave for nine months and authored many of the Book of Psalms while on his tunnel faith journey. The more significant outcome of tunnel Faith is that our Lord will perform great works in you when you come out of your tunnel faith season. David's outcome was to become the second King of Israel.

Spiritual Blinders (Blinkers) is one way we ought to operate in this strategic approach: to block out all the distractions to hear the voice of God through an assignment. This strategic approach keeps you focused on the assignment.

Reflection Time

Have you found yourself practicing the Tunnel Faith strategy in the last couple of months? If so, how has it been?

_____

Chapter 3: Mustard Seed Faith

As I was embarking on this part of the book, I was looking for some guidance or a super powerful encounter in the middle of the night. But we can apply mustard seed, which can be occupied at any moment. Mustard seed faith is something we tend to obtain in our everyday lives. Remember the first time you felt the presence of our Lord. Remember a time when you knew that it was our Father who moved on your behalf. Do you remember when you prayed to our Father about a particular situation, and within 24 hours, there was a turnaround? (that you know that your own God could do).

Let us go through such a classical and rooted principle in our daily walk as a servant. How could something so small be a representation of something so massive?

Our Lord is so clever and wise. Comparing such a thing is a wonderful seed. Mustard Seeds are known to be the smallest living seed in the world. After viewing it, I realized this could not produce something of great magnitude. I see a mustard seed as the weight of a handful of unsweetened white sugar. Some would say that unsweetened sugar has no weight, but when you are holding a handful, it has some weight. It is powerful enough to bring such an excellent taste to any entrée. That is the same thing with mustard seeds. I was amazed that when you plant a mustard seed, you do not have to put several seeds into one pot to make it grow. So, what better way to get you to understand how important it is to know and embrace your mustard seed faith on your journey.

Here is a revelation you can obtain from this:

1. Mustard seeds are tiny but, with proper care, can grow to six feet tall. So do not deny yourself the benefit of growth in your faith. It may not be where you want it now, but you will grow.

2. Mustard seeds are symbolic of the potential of Faith. Jesus talked about Mustard seeds several times in the gospels. He knows his children and believes in us.

3. Mustard seeds must be watered regularly to avoid pests. To live a Christ-like lifestyle, you will need to feed your spiritual being through his word and avoid distractions and/or self-sabotage that stop your growth in the Lord.

The Power of the Mustard Seed Faith

A Roman Centurion who was held to ambitious standards and was over soldiers had an encounter that changed the life of his servant. The Roman Centurion heard of the miracle signs and wonders that Jesus Christ had performed and had a servant who needed to be healed. Jesus Christ's presence alone brought a change in someone who was known as a servant to the Roman Army. I knew that Jesus Christ could heal. His faith was unwavering. So unwavering that during the conservation with Jesus, the Centurion knew the magnitude of his presence. The Centurion's unwavering faith shows the depths of just belief. Jesus asked the Centurion," Shall I come and heal him?" (Matthew 8:7).

The response of the Roman Centurion in the bible was humbling but powerful. This moment reminds us of how nothing is impossible for our Lord. Our father is so kind that he looks at the heart of people. Although the Roman Centurion knew his status and where he stood, he also knew the power of Jesus Christ. An army commander demonstrated the power of the Mustard seed Faith. Later in the scripture, Jesus says, "Truly I tell you; I have not found anyone in Israel with such great faith."

*(Matthew 8:10).

Matthew 8:5-13
"5 When Jesus had entered Capernaum, a centurion came to him, asking for help. 6 "Lord," he said, "my servant lies at home paralyzed, suffering terribly."7 Jesus said to him, "Shall I come and heal him?"8 The centurion replied, "Lord, I do not deserve to have you come under my roof. But say the word and my servant will be healed. 9 For I am a man under authority, with soldiers under me. I tell this one, 'Go,' and he goes; and that one, 'Come,' and he comes. I tell my servant, 'Do this,' and he does it."10 When Jesus heard this, he was amazed and said to those following him, "Truly I tell you, I have not found anyone in Israel with such great faith. 11 I say to you that many will come from the east and the west and will take their places at the feast with Abraham, Isaac, and Jacob in the kingdom of heaven. 12 But the kingdom's subjects will be thrown outside, into the darkness, where there will be weeping and gnashing of teeth."13 Then Jesus said to the centurion, "Go! Let it be done just as you believed it would." And his servant was healed at that moment." NIV

Move the Mountain Faith

So, how does a tiny seed, such as a mustard seed, compare to a mountain? Jesus Christ was such a great teacher and was always in a place to bring realization of the importance of drawing closer to Our Father during his time on Earth. His divine instructions were so relevant, but sometimes not understood by the people around him unless they were in a place to thrive, seeking a newness that only God could provide. If you are like me, Jesus' parables were everything, and his confidence was so unwavering. What a great mentor!!! Faith was so easy to obtain, and access was free. Just think if you believe that it could move mountains as the smallest seed in the world. My LORD!! Hallelujah. This is great for us. How can you fail? It is a win/ win lifestyle.

Application Time

Matthew 13:31-32
Jesus used another illustration: "The Kingdom of Heaven is like a mustard seed planted in a field. 32 It is the smallest of all seeds, but it becomes the largest of garden plants; it grows into a tree, and birds come and make nests in its branches."
   You are a part of the kingdom now, and here is your time to practice and bring full engagement to your journey. Know that your faith will grow, and your faith will help bring others to the body of Christ. NLT

Matthew 17:20
20 He replied, "Because you have so little faith. Truly I tell you, if you have faith as small as a mustard seed, you can say to this mountain, 'Move from here to there,' and it will move. Nothing will be impossible for you. NIV

Here is your first chance to trust the process and believe that with Faith, there is nothing impossible for our Lord to do. Even your most significant hurdle(challenge) if you reach for it. (Faith wave.) What is something you believe in in your life right now? Something that a man would say is not possible. Decree and declare that your situation will be dealt with according to the will of the Father.

_____

_____

_____

_____

_____

_____

_____

_____

Mark 4:31-32
It is like a mustard seed planted in the ground. Although it is the smallest seed, it becomes the largest of all garden plants; it grows long branches, and birds can make nests in its shade. NLT

Mustard Seed Faith, if watered correctly, becomes the largest plant, so reflect on this. You have presented your situation to our Father, and now you are applying what the word says. How has your situation changed since you challenged yourself through the Declaration?

_____

_____

_____

_____

_____

_____

_____

_____

Let me remind you that your application of your Faith is critical to your growth in your Faith Walk. Here is scripture to encourage you to again preserve Mustard Seed Faith, which, if watered correctly, becomes the largest plant, so reflect on this. You have presented your situation to our God, and now you are applying what the word says.

Luke 17:6
6 And the Lord said, "If you had faith like a grain of mustard seed, you could say to this mulberry tree, 'Be uprooted and planted in the sea,' and it would obey you. KJV

Chapter 4: Miraculous Faith

We want to define Miraculous. I purposely use the adjective definition of miraculous because I want to bring an understanding that it is a description of an action. Miraculous Faith is defined as "occurring through a divine or supernatural intervention." There have been many testimonies of Miraculous faith, and many would say this is the hardest to engage in without the belief system of knowing who our Father would have us and what he is. There have been many encounters throughout the bible; we can now witness and experience our Father's wonders. Many of you who read this book have heard of accounts or have had your own experiences. One question I would like to raise is about your encounter with your miraculous faith.

Reflection: Oil Jars

2 Kings 4:1-7
"One day, the widow of a member of the group of prophets came to Elisha and cried out, "My husband who served you is dead, and you know how he feared the Lord. But now a creditor has come, threatening to take my two sons as slaves."2 "What can I do to help you?" Elisha asked. "Tell me, what do you have in the house?" "Nothing at all, except a flask of olive oil," she replied.3 And Elisha said, "Borrow as many empty jars as you can from your friends and neighbors. 4 Then go into your house with your sons and shut the door behind you. Pour olive oil from your flask into the jars, setting each one aside when it is filled."5 So she did as she was told. Her sons kept bringing jars to her, and she filled one after another. 6 Soon every container was full to the brim! "Bring me another jar," she said to one of her sons. "There aren't any more!" he told her. And then the olive oil stopped flowing.7 When she told the man of God what had

happened, he said to her, "Now sell the olive oil and pay your debts, and you and your sons can live on what is left over." NLT

Personal Moment A- Encounter

I am reminded of a moment of miraculous faith.

One day, I woke up, and I was fine. I went about doing my daily routine, as usual. Within two hours after our morning prayer, I noticed that my head had begun to hurt a little. I understood it maybe because I needed some caffeine due to lack of sleep. So, I convinced myself to lie down, and I will pray more when I get back up. Boy, was I completely wrong for going to sleep at all. Before lying down, I got up and started praising God by singing and dancing. The pain was disappearing the more I sang his praises.

Now, let me go back to the moment I went to sleep. I woke up feeling even worse. Bam, I realized while I was asleep that I was being spiritually attacked. What was a small amount of pain becoming unbearable. It was like someone was crawling in my head with heels on. My eyes were so sensitive. I woke up and started to rock myself in a fetal position. So, I knew I needed to call reinforcements. I petition my children to start praying for me. Desperate, I went into my prayer language and cried out to

Jesus. "Jesus Help," Lord, please take this pain away. Tears ran down my face, and my body was tense then. I became numb.

Then came the turning point. After the cry-out moment (Calling Jesus for healing), a message was received that healing would occur. I closed my eyes and rolled over on my back. But wait! My daughter came into the room and told me Ma, look at your environment. (For those who know me, I have a certain environment that I am always in). (She mentions you typically have a specific sound in your area and usually wear certain items when fighting spiritual attacks. This is not a typical worship environment for the Lord to come into your environment.) Now, stay with me. This is all going to make sense. *** So, I changed my atmosphere quickly, put my worship playlist on, and set my atmosphere for the presence of the Lord to come into the place. "Now, back to our regular programming."

This is when the healing began to take place. Now, the encounter was miraculous. Some of you have heard about healing encounters or may have even experienced them. It started with a warm sensation going up my face around my nose, traveling to my ears, and onto the front of my forehead.it felt like someone was pulling off something around my forehead from the left to right side. My body was like a thermostat that was put on to a hot burning. I began to sweat, but in this encounter, I noticed everything I felt was warm in one part of my face; I would feel the pain in another part of my head. Within twenty minutes, I was in a deep sleep.

While sleeping, I felt something pulling out of my forehead and the back of my head. Along my ears as well. About an hour later, I woke up feeling better. I lay there and thanked the Lord for his healing power. I was able to think again. I felt the release of my forehead area. I sat up and felt an out-of-body experience. So, I lay back down. Healing was still taking place. I am still amazed and grateful for the healing. I lay there and told myself I would stay in bed a little longer. Within ten minutes, I had a strange feeling of nausea, and I got up very quickly and ran to the bathroom. After throwing up twice, I returned to my bed and tried to lie but could not. So, I decided to sit in a different location. I got my blanket and sat up, sleeping. When I woke up, thirty minutes later. I was completely healed with no signs of pain in my body. My Father is so good. Once again, he came and healed me. He rescues me from the hands of the enemy.

I give him praise, Lord, thank you.

Insight from a Miraculous Faith

Come with me as I walk you through a time of revelation about Miraculous Faith. One of Jesus' first miracles was at a celebration of a union.

John 2:1-11
The next day there was a wedding celebration in the village of Cana in Galilee. Jesus' mother was there, 2 and Jesus and his disciples were also invited to the celebration. 3 The wine supply ran out during the festivities, so Jesus' mother told him, "They have no more wine."4 "Dear woman, that's not our problem," Jesus replied. "My time has not yet come."5 But his mother told the servants, "Do whatever he tells you."6 Standing nearby were six stone water jars, used for Jewish ceremonial washing. Each could hold twenty to thirty gallons.7 Jesus told the servants, "Fill the jars with water." When the jars had been filled, 8 he said, "Now dip some out, and take it to the master of ceremonies." So, the servants followed his instructions 9 When the master of ceremonies tasted the water that was now wine, not knowing where it had come from (though, of course, the servants knew), he called the bridegroom over. 10 "A host always serves the best wine first," he said. "Then, when everyone has had a lot to drink, he brings out the less expensive wine. But you have kept the best until now!"11 This miraculous sign at Cana in Galilee was the first time Jesus revealed his glory. And his disciples believed in him. NLT

The confidence that his mother had in him to perform what was inside of him was a "given moment." This was Jesus's first miracle. The outcome was the belief of his disciples and the activation of more miracles to come. Our Lord shows so much grace.

Chapter 5: Victorious Through Our Faith

You are a walking testimony. The things you have been through clearly indicate that God is working it out for you. Our God is fighting on your behalf. That your progress in your life is because of his increase. As you go through every assignment, there will be an outpour of testimonies, spiritual confidence, and spiritual growth, whether you know it or not. Here is a biblical insight into how meaningful your desire should be in walking closely with our Lord throughout your life. Being obedient to the Lord's instructions is especially important to have victory through Faith.

This is a familiar passage, but it reveals so much about victory through faith in God. Joshua was a great soldier and later became a leader of a nation. He led the Israelites out of the wilderness into the promised land. Joshua's confidence was built on the sure fact that the Lord would guide him and give him instructions to win through Faith and victory, from sending spies to the city beforehand to the present strategy.

Many people read this passage and did not realize some interesting fact about this assignment that the Lord has Joshua on. First, let us bring some revelation about the size of Jericho. Growing up, I always assumed that Jericho was a small town. In Sunday school, we were never taught the details of Jericho or the significance of the details of the instructions given to Joshua. Pause for a minute.... (Build your relationship with God)

So, as you grow and become more aware of the Lord's presence, you will hear his instructions for you in your welcome basket. He will give you step-by-step instructions; he will give you some details. Our challenge is to follow, hear his voice and when all else fails. Just be obedient. In the story of Joshua, the Lord, and Joshua had built a solid relationship, and his confidence was high because he ultimately trusted God. The revelation in this pause moment is that you must develop your relationship with God.

I wouldn't compare our relationship with God to earthly relationships... because this relationship is significant. However, what is similar is that with any relationship, if you love a person or want to build trust in the relationship, you must engage in it. Our relationship with God is, above all, the most crucial entity in our complete existence.

1. Jericho was a massive kingdom—not a county, city, or kingdom. According to archaeological evidence, it was estimated to be around 430,000 square feet.

2. Joshua was given specific instructions on how many days he and his fighting soldiers would walk around the walls.

3. Numerical insight was significant to the assignment. Numbers such as 7 mean completeness or fullness. Joshua was told to have seven priests walk with ram horns in front of the Ark Covenant (blowing the horns) and was instructed to walk around the walls. On the seventh time around, shout aloud.

The story of Joshua leading the Israelites to bring down the walls of Jericho is a powerful account that demonstrates the Lord's faithfulness and might. This narrative fulfills God's greater promise to the Israelites that they would indeed enter the Promised Land.

Joshua 6:1-20
Now Jericho was straitly shut up because of the children of Israel: none went out, and none came in.² And the LORD said unto Joshua, See, I have given into thine hand Jericho, and the king thereof, and the mighty men of valour.³ And ye shall compass the city, all ye men of war, and go round about the city once. Thus shalt thou do six days.⁴ And seven priests shall bear before the ark seven trumpets of rams' horns: and the seventh day ye shall compass the city seven times, and the priests shall blow with the trumpets.⁵ And it shall come to pass, that when they make a long blast with the ram's horn, and when ye hear the

sound of the trumpet, all the people shall shout with a great shout; and the wall of the city shall fall down flat, and the people shall ascend up every man straight before him. [6] And Joshua the son of Nun called the priests, and said unto them, Take up the ark of the covenant, and let seven priests bear seven trumpets of rams' horns before the ark of the LORD. [7] And he said unto the people, Pass on, and compass the city, and let him that is armed pass on before the ark of the LORD. [8] And it came to pass, when Joshua had spoken unto the people, that the seven priests bearing the seven trumpets of rams' horns passed on before the LORD, and blew with the trumpets: and the ark of the covenant of the LORD followed them. [9] And the armed men went before the priests that blew with the trumpets, and the rereward came after the ark, the priests going on, and blowing with the trumpets. [10] And Joshua had commanded the people, saying, Ye shall not shout, nor make any noise with your voice, neither shall any word proceed out of your mouth, until the day I bid you shout; then shall ye shout. [11] So the ark of the LORD compassed the city, going about it once: and they came into the camp, and lodged in the camp. [12] And Joshua rose early in the morning, and the priests took up the ark of the LORD. [13] And seven priests bearing seven trumpets of rams' horns before the ark of the LORD went on continually, and blew with the trumpets: and the armed men went before them; but the rereward came after the ark of the LORD, the priests going on, and blowing with the trumpets. [14] And the second day they compassed the city once, and returned into the camp: so they did six days. [15] And it came to pass on the seventh day, that they rose early about the dawning of the day, and compassed the city after the same manner seven times: only on that day they compassed the city seven times. [16] And it came to pass at the seventh time, when the priests blew with the trumpets, Joshua said unto the people, Shout; for the LORD hath given you the city. [17] And the city shall be accursed, even it, and all that are therein, to the LORD: only Rahab the harlot shall live, she and all that are with her in the house, because she hid the messengers that we sent. [18] And ye, in any wise keep yourselves from the accursed thing, lest ye make yourselves accursed, when ye take of the accursed thing, and make the camp of Israel a curse, and trouble it. [19] But all the silver, and gold, and vessels of brass and iron, are consecrated unto the LORD: they shall come into the treasury of the LORD. [20] So the people shouted when the priests blew with the trumpets: and it came to pass, when the people heard the sound of the trumpet, and the people shouted with a great shout, that the wall fell down flat, so that the people went up into the city, every man straight before him, and they took the city. KJV

Chapter 6: Growth In Your Faith

Now it is your turn. You have navigated through this book, and now it is time for your faith to grow higher. In spiritual growth, Faith should increase to higher heights. "I have fought the good fight, I have finished the race, I have kept the faith." 2 Timothy 4:7-8. Our goal is to completely trust our Lord and walk out the Lord's divine purpose for us through faith.

My Faith has been tested.

Now, there is a particular show that I grew up with emphasizing reading and knowledge, and it would come on every week on Saturday morning before it came and had this very classical, um up inspiring, uplifting intro. In the intro, when you were watching it visually, it had a rainbow and butterflies and all this gooey happiness that was going on, and it did not get me wrong; reading is fundamental. And it is so crucial because knowledge is power. The host of the TV show would have presented content, and throughout the show, there was always some conflict that was brought out to be answered. By the end of the show, they found options to solve the conflict that was present during the show—and always concluded with the theme song of hope.

This is what happens in your faith walk. We come into the body of Christ with complete trust in knowing he is our Savior. You start going through seasons where your faith is being tested. Guess what? You are on the right track.

James 1:2-4

[2] My brethren, count it all joy when ye fall into divers temptations;[3] Knowing this, that the trying of your faith worketh patience.[4] But let patience have her perfect work, that ye may be perfect and entire, wanting nothing.KJV

My faith has been tested in many ways throughout my journey in Christ. One thing that remains the same is that the Lord is always with me. He never put more on us than we can bear. Throughout your journey, you will learn that applying faith is very important. Let's look at it two ways. In some cases, you realize you were stronger than you thought. In some situations, you know that the Lord moved on your behalf and just brought you to the awareness of how much your faith has grown.

So yes, you are now aware of the difficulties in our faith journey. As you grow, so will your faith and how it is challenged. And if you have not felt the fire yet, trust and believe you will experience some growth pains. With growth pains come more accountability, awareness, and the courage to progress in your walk with Christ.

Spiritual Warfare

Just like a parent with a newborn, you will do anything to protect your baby, and later realize that as they grow into adults, our level of protection is different. At any time, what was so easy when they were babies to protect and conquer, now they are in adulthood, your response is to preserve and destroy. But they must learn to make it applicable independently, and you must know that you have done everything you can to give them. They need to be sustained in their journey, which is the same thing regarding faith.

As much as we do not want to acknowledge that as we evolved in faith, spiritual warfare became more evident. The sooner we are abreast of it, the smoother it will be for us to equip ourselves for the journey. There will be more to encounter, and we are compelled to be conscious of the realization that Faith cultivates growth.

Coming into Christ, the Lord sustains us and models us to levels of Faith. At full length, he protects us and aligns us by building our character.

Romans 5:3-4.

[3] And not only so, but we glory in tribulations also: knowing that tribulation worketh patience;[4] And patience, experience; and experience, hope: KJV

Our Lord believes so much, even when we cannot believe in ourselves. He gives us full access to wisdom and boldness in our faith journey. The Lord wants us to flourish. Being tested through our trials and tribulations will cultivate our ability to navigate despite everything. Growth is the direct product of our faith, and the Lord grants us an immeasurable outpouring.

John 16:33
"I have told you these things so that you may have peace in me. In this world, you will have trouble. But take heart! I have overcome the world NLT

Chapter 7: Faith Wave

A wave is defined as a surge of sensation or emotion, which leads me to bring the revelation of the unique moment of Faith. Faith waves can be classified as a surge of sensation. We have these moments when miracles are performed. When something unexpected happens, you know it could not be anything but the Lord himself that made a way or made it happen. I am reminded of a healing that took place in the Bible. It would be wrong of me not to share some of the most inspired Faith moments in the Bible. As you read these scriptures, see who you have similarities with and where you fit in your walk-through Faith. Remember, this book is meant to give you the resources to apply to your everyday walk with Jesus.

1. <u>If I can get to him....</u>

I wrote a message about a familiar passage in the Bible back in 2023. Come travel with me during this grateful moment.

"I woke up this morning in a spirit of gratefulness to Jesus. I woke up hopeful and began to tear up. I was astonished and honestly just grateful to be awake once again. The power of my Father Jesus is demonstrated and must be brought into the awareness and understanding of how important Faith is. Faithfulness is so essential and relevant in our lives. So, in the three Gospels of the New Testament, the outcome is still the same for all three books in the New Testament. She was made whole.

Matthew 9:20-22 NIV

Just then, a woman who had been subject to bleeding for twelve years came up behind him and touched the edge of his cloak. 21 She said to herself, "If I only touch his cloak, I will be healed."
22 Jesus turned and saw her. "Take heart, daughter," he said, "your faith has healed you." And the woman was healed at that moment.
Mark 5:25-34 NIV

And a woman was there who had been subject to bleeding for twelve years. 26 She had suffered a great deal under the care of many doctors and had spent all she had, yet instead of getting better she grew worse. 27 When she heard about Jesus, she came up behind him in the crowd and touched his cloak, 28 because she thought, "If I just touch his clothes, I will be healed." 29 Immediately her bleeding stopped and she felt in her body that she was freed from her suffering. 30 At once Jesus realized that power had gone out from him. He turned around in the crowd and asked, "Who touched my clothes?" 31 "You see the people crowding against you," his disciples answered, "yet you can ask, 'Who touched me?' " 32 But Jesus kept looking around to see who had done it. 33 Then the woman, knowing what had happened to her, came and fell at his feet and, trembling with fear, told him the whole truth. 34 He told her, "Daughter, your Faith has healed you. Go in peace and be freed from your suffering."

Luke 8:43-48NIV

43 And a woman was there who had been subject to bleeding for twelve years, [a] but no one could heal her. 44 She came up behind him and touched the edge of his cloak, and immediately her bleeding stopped. 45 "Who touched me?" Jesus asked. When they all denied it, Peter said, "Master, the people are crowding and pressing against you." 46 But Jesus said, "Someone touched me; I know that power has gone out from me." 47 Then the woman, seeing that she could not go unnoticed, came trembling and fell at his feet. In the presence of all the people, she told why she had touched him and how she had been instantly healed. 48 Then he said to her, "Daughter, your Faith has healed you. Go in peace."

The most essential part of all three versions is her journey, a remarkable story about the importance of determination and hope. Faith was exercised, and the outcome was growth.

In that quick moment, I was reminded of my situation. I went on vacation for a couple of days and returned feeling energetic and motivated. My day was filled with a couple of meetings, and I finished my day off with thoughts of resting. But I was on a faith wave and continued to press on until the following day, "Bam!' The pain I was feeling was not like any other. It may seem like I am exaggerating, but I could not even think. My whole body was feeling all types of pain. This pain came unexpectedly; I was operating through our daily routine and continued to press through the pain even though it worsened. Experience my pain in quietness. I continue to proceed and believe that this, too, shall pass. As my husband and children make their way through, my oldest daughter glances at me and notices that there is a tremendous amount of pain coming from my facial expression.

Trying to be the overcomer that I am, I maneuver in everyday engagement, hoping that I could throw her off. "I will be alright" is something I speak to decree and declare healing over myself. She confidently agreed with me by saying, "Maybe it's your sinuses; it looks like it's going to rain?" I replied, holding on to the confidence that this moment of pain was going to subside. Agony crept up and took complete control; the rest of my body followed what would later be called a "spiritual attack." I became victim to the pain, and even after praying a couple of times, I followed it up with some medicine decree that in an hour or so, I would be back on my feet.

Time passed, and what was an hour was now half an hour in the afternoon. By then, I had taken off my armor of God and was on the verge of taking that "L" confidently. Rationalizing some options, I realized that I could not do it alone and called for reinforcement. The scriptures say when two or three are gathered in his name, our Father is in the mist. I could not believe it. The enemy got a blow on me; how was this possible? "How do you go on vacation?" to lying in bed wondering when I could get up. Now, in complete darkness, after my husband came to speak life and healing into me. I lay there defeated. There were moments of perseverance, but it was derailed several times throughout the day. Tossed to and from, I submitted to the pain and cried out to God, "Help!"

And I was reminded about the woman with the issue of blood. Her story was much longer than my moment. Three accounts in the Bible mention her story. The woman with the issue of blood was immune to her issue but still sought to find a way to overcome her issue. She heard of a man from Galilee ministering healing and delivery throughout the land. She pressed her way there, although being amongst the people with her issue was forbidden. Have you ever been where the woman with the issue of blood had been? Have you ever just had enough and cried to the Lord, "HELP!"

You just read the scriptures, and you know the outcome. Through this woman's desperation, there comes a point that nothing will change her mind about encountering Jesus. And if that meant that she was compelled to crawl to touch the hem of his garment. The woman with the issue of blood determination produced a great outcome. She reaches for the Messiah's garment, and the scriptures say he felt some of his power was

41

gone. He looked around, trying to see where it came from, but later, he realized that the woman with the issue of blood had admitted to the action of Faith. Our Father is so fantastic and blessed her. "Your Faith has made you whole. Go in Peace."

An awakening rose in me at about 7 pm, and I figured that if I could call on the name of the Lord, I would be healed. The woman with the issue of the Blood story was a reminder to me and sprung forth some buried Faith. I rose up and called my husband to help me sit in my chair. We administered some peppermints, and I anchored my legs. And like the woman with the issue of blood, I fought my way to the healer. I kept repositioning myself until I fell asleep in my Father's presence.

I woke up at 10 pm with my body completely healed. Our Jesus came through and healed my body. I crawled my way through and preserved it. Because of my Faith and determination, I was healed. Our Father is a healer, Jehovah Rapha. I even woke up wanting to eat but decided to wait until the next day to consume some food.

Here is the revelation: Faith Wave came to the woman with the issue of blood through her determination and Faith. The more significant outcome was her miraculous healing through activating her Faith in our Father. Some people would say that it does not take all that, but I say it takes all that. This story is a perfect example of Faith being in action. Many of you, including me, can glance upon this moment and recharge yourself when your Faith is being tried.

Sometimes, you must remind yourself to reposition your look or actions of Faith in your Father. He is there and cares for you. Whatever it takes for you to focus on your Faith, engage with boldness. YOU ARE NOW WHOLE.

Journal Moment B

December 31, 2024

Hello again. I am here and in a different place than when I started this journey. I would have to say that the space I am in now is…… "Lord, I am your servant." What does that mean? This year has been a year for me, fighting to understand why the Lord would want me to travel down a road that seems so unsure. In all my years of serving him. I have engaged in some wonderful assignments. However, some problematic tasks may have come with them. I was firm that I just wanted to please my father. It was so easy to engage in something that was so freely comfortable and had the knowledge to embrace the process. But when it got hard, the very thing that I felt weak in was the same thing the Lord brought me back to. I would never have thought I would be back down this road. I left these moments in my younger days, and as Life 101 presented itself, I replaced them with moments that seemed much easier.

Do not get me wrong, being a servant is the most embedded lifestyle (moment) without any thought or struggle to engage in. However, the different realms were never brought to my attention until I had to come back to a place that I felt was not supposed to carve another moment when I realized that dreams do not equal reality. Life 101 was a distant memory as I walked into Life 102. Now I am here dancing thoughts on a doc form, hoping that what was once a dream will be confirmed by my Lord as reality. As a human, as a mother, as a wife, as a business owner, but more than anything, as a servant. I am honored that our Lord sought to allow me to grace my thoughts and bring awareness of how vital your resources and guidance are. Lord is everything. Lord, you are all known; we want to progress with you. Your word was presented to equip us to be key instruments (tools) in helping the movement of Hope. God's kingdom is granted to everyone, and he has prepared unlimited resources and instructions for you to succeed.

So now I am here. I am here, Lord, about to free fall in this reality that was once a dream. You believe in me so much. I can let my thoughts of being weak take the place of your word that declares and empowers us to run to you for strength. (When I am weak Lord, you are strong scripture.) Lord, here I am. Thank you for allowing the Holy Spirit to be with us. Thank you for seeing that we are worth serving you and representing you.

Faith without work is dead.

Journal Moment C

Jan. 17, 2025

Here is your turn now. God has called you for an assignment that will take the next step or level of faith he has entrusted you to walk into. You have grown; now it is time to walk into new territories. It is time to establish your feet in places that the Lord has equipped you to bring change (his word into the atmosphere). You are his representative. You are appointed. Allow his anointing to consume you and speak to him to the nations. He will give you the words to say; they will be so clear that a child can understand them. The words he gives you will transform his people. It will bring refreshment to the weary and bring deliverance to the wanderers. Do not think about it; just be obedient to the call. Your faith has been assessed, and you are ready for the most significant assignment.

Our Father is wonderful, and he always knows what is best for us. Although Abraham was a great man of Faith, the Lord showed Abraham the importance of full trust in him. Abraham's passion for God had so much depth because of his faithfulness to God. The Lord blessed him to be the Father of many nations. His favor is demonstrated generation after generation.

That is the same thing that our Father wants to do for us. He has full hope in us to do right, and his unconditional love never becomes conditional, no matter what we do or how we lack.

Chapter 8: Walk on Water Faith

At the beginning of 2024, I presented a message to a ministry we partner with, "Walk on Water." This is a classic story in the Bible about an encounter between Jesus and one of the disciples, Peter. This moment alone was revelational about the sovereign presence of Jesus Christ. The response of this moment awakened the disciples of Jesus Christ, the coming King, our Messiah.

Matthew 14:22-31

[22] And straightway Jesus constrained his disciples to get into a ship, and to go before him unto the other side, while he sent the multitudes away. [23] And when he had sent the multitudes away, he went up into a mountain apart to pray: and when the evening was come, he was there alone. [24] But the ship was now in the midst of the sea, tossed with waves: for the wind was contrary. [25] And in the fourth watch of the night Jesus went unto them, walking on the sea. [26] And when the disciples saw him walking on the sea, they were troubled, saying, It is a spirit; and they cried out for fear. [27] But straightway Jesus spake unto them, saying, Be of good cheer; it is I; be not afraid. [28] And Peter answered him and said, Lord, if it be thou, bid me come unto thee on the water. [29] And he said, Come. And when Peter was come down out of the ship, he walked on the water, to go to Jesus. [30] But when he saw the wind boisterous, he was afraid; and beginning to sink, he cried, saying, Lord, save me. [31] And immediately Jesus stretched forth his hand, and caught him, and said unto him, O thou of little faith, wherefore didst thou doubt? KJV

Mark 6: 45-51

[45] And straightway he constrained his disciples to get into the ship, and to go to the other side before unto Bethsaida, while he sent away the people. [46] And when he had sent them away, he departed into a mountain to pray. [47] And when even was come, the ship was in the midst of the sea, and he alone on the land. [48] And

he saw them toiling in rowing; for the wind was contrary unto them: and about the fourth watch of the night he cometh unto them, walking upon the sea, and would have passed by them.[49] But when they saw him walking upon the sea, they supposed it had been a spirit, and cried out:[50] For they all saw him, and were troubled. And immediately he talked with them, and saith unto them, Be of good cheer: it is I; be not afraid.[51] And he went up unto them into the ship; and the wind ceased: and they were sore amazed in themselves beyond measure, and wondered.

John 6:16-21 NLT
16 That evening Jesus' disciples went down to the shore to wait for him. 17 But as darkness fell and Jesus still hadn't come back, they got into the boat and headed across the lake toward Capernaum. 18 Soon a gale swept down upon them, and the sea grew very rough. 19 They had rowed three or four miles when suddenly they saw Jesus walking on the water toward the boat. They were terrified, 20 but he called out to them, "Don't be afraid. I am here! " 21 Then they were eager to let him in the boat, and immediately they arrived at their destination!

Peter trusted Jesus. Peter saw Jesus do miracles, signs, and wonders. Peter was loyal and wanted to show Jesus, he would follow him wherever he went. That is how we should be when it comes to trusting the Father in our lives. In the body of Christ, we have all experienced some assignments requiring faith levels. And now you are in a place(season) where Jesus is calling you.

You were like Peter. You said, "Jesus, all I will go," and you walked in the water. As the storms and things started getting uncomfortable in your assignment. You began to sing. Jesus come and lifted you up to encourage you today to keep pressing towards the mark.

Don't take your eyes off Jesus. There will be times when you feel alone. There may be times when you may not get the support you need. Hold on and focus on walking to Jesus. He got you. Because of Peter's obedience, He continues his journey with the Lord. His Love was great for Jesus. Peter's names mean "Rock". Peter later became an Apostle and formed many other churches. The Lord will do the same for you.

Your obedience will bring victory reports and enhancement in the kingdom. The season is now. Jesus calls you to take a considerable leap into the water and come to him. He's got you. So, it depends on where you are. Maybe the Lord told you to start a business a while ago, but you have been waiting for your instructions. The Lord is waiting for you to step forth. Your walk on water faith can apply to many things in your life. Please know that these moments exist in your faith walk in the Lord.

Jude 1:20

20 *But ye, beloved, building up yourselves on your most holy faith, praying in the Holy Ghost, KJV*

Application Time #1

This message is for you if you have not experienced anything in this new year. If there have been obstacles in your new year, this message is for you, too. No matter where you are in your walk with Christ, this classic story teaches us the importance of faith. If you are like me, here is a creative way to remember the principle of Faith.

Reference Scripture: Hebrews 12:2

"Fixing our eyes on Jesus, the pioneer and perfecter of faith. For the joy set before him, he endured the cross, scorning its shame, and sat down at the right hand of the throne of God." NIV

F: Foundation

Romans 1:17
For in the gospel, the righteousness of God is revealed—a righteousness that is by faith from first to last, just as it is written: "The righteous will live by faith. NIV

The most remarkable man of faith was our Father, Jesus. Jesus operated in who he was and even spoke to us to show us how to cultivate Faith. We started our faith journey by accepting him and understanding how important Jesus Christ must be.

A: Actions

As we begin to walk fluently on what the word says, how and why we need to live a certain way. We realize that we cannot achieve it with our Lord. We began to practice through actions what the word says we are and how to live in him. Through actions, our faith grows. We gain momentum from trusting the Lord through our everyday lives. We then began to respond to the will of the Father by the instructions he gave us.

James 2:26
Faith without work is dead. NIV
James 2:14-26
What good is it, my brothers and sisters, if someone claims to have faith but has no deeds? Can such faith save them? 15 Suppose a brother or a sister is without clothes and daily food. 16 If one of you says to them, "Go in peace; keep warm and well fed," but does nothing about their physical needs, what good is it? 17 Similarly, faith by itself, if it is not accompanied by action, is dead.18 Someone will say, "You have faith; I have deeds. "Show me your faith without deeds, and I will show you my faith by my deeds. 19 You believe that there is one God. Good! Even the demons believe that—and shudder.20 You foolish person, do you want evidence that faith without deeds is useless 21 Was our father Abraham not considered righteous for what he did when he offered his son Isaac on the altar? 22 You see that his faith and actions were working together, and his faith was made complete by what he did. 23 And the scripture was fulfilled that says, "Abraham believed God, and it was credited to him as righteousness," and he was called God's friend. 24 You see that a person is considered righteous by what they do and not by faith alone. NIV

You must put some work in as the Lord gives you instructions.

One thing that remains the same is that actions respond to that faith. Our eyes are fixed on the Lord and his orders on our steps. As we conquer each assignment, he builds us up in response to our trust in our Lord. Faith. We believe and take strength in that.

Hebrews 11:1
Faith is confidence in what we hope for and assurance about what we do not see. KJV

I: Ignite catches fire or causes it to catch fire. (Verb)

In Faith, the I, although are the three letters. It is essential to understand that it is the beginning of our walk with Christ. Once we receive the Lord. There is something inside of us that gets turned on. For example, when you make a fire at a camp, once you turn that pilot onto the gas and it touches the wood, it spreads quickly and brightly. It becomes light once we are concerned with darkness, and when we receive (Lord), the Lord ignites us, his marvelous light (our Lord).

Reading his words makes you realize that growth takes place through actions, and when obstacles come, you know that the Lord has empowered you. You begin to not just act and ignite but respond to what his words say. Your faith increases... Boldness and engagement in scriptures like Philippians 4:13 become an anthem for you and the Lord's promises he has for you.

Philippians 4:13
I can do all this through him, who gives **me strength. KJV**
Matthew 17:20-21
He replied, "Because you have so little faith. Truly I tell you, if you have faith as small as a mustard seed, you can say to this mountain, 'Move from here to there,' and it will move. Nothing will be impossible for you. NIV
2 Corinthians. 5:7
For we live by faith, not by sight. NIV
H: HIM (Hope Ful)

Our Savior is the hope dealer. There is fullness in him when we draw near to him. Now that you know more about FAITH, can you honestly say that you are living fully through all the letters?

Do you sometimes miss spelling the word faith through our lifestyles?

ROMANS 10:17
Consequently, faith comes from hearing the message, which is heard through the word about Christ. NIV
1 Corinthians 12:7-11
Now, to each one, the manifestation of the Spirit is given for the common good. 8 To one there is given through the Spirit a message of wisdom, to another a message of knowledge by means of the same Spirit, 9 to another faith by the same Spirit, to another gift of healing by that one Spirit, 10 to another miraculous powers, to another prophecy, to another distinguishing between spirits, to another speaking in different kinds of tongues, and to still another the interpretation of tongues. 11 All these are the work of one and the same Spirit, and he distributes them to each one, just as he determines. NIV

Application Time #2 In the Eye of the Storm

There have been a lot of things going on, including the goals that we set for our family and ourselves. We see God moving, we see ourselves growing, and we move forward on what God called us to do. Life has its difficulties. We know that Jesus will be with us. His words say this to be true. We keep pressing and working through, focusing on our God.

In 2024, a tornado hit our area two weeks before Christmas. Here is the encounter that took place.

Recently, I went to the store and got something. My daughter asked me about going to the hair store since we were out. So, there is a particular store she goes to, but we were in a different part of the town. So, we had to drive down this long road. So, I had not been on that road for a while. As I was driving, things looked familiar, and then I noticed a vast area still being destroyed by a tornado that hit us right a couple of weeks before Christmas.

My daughter and I looked with shock, and I said, "Wait, I thought they cleaned up the area?" Still shocked by what we saw, everything on one side of the road was gone, except for the white house in the center, which was not touched, but everything around it was gone. This white house was not brick; it was built mostly with wood and had a brick chimney.

During this same season, I had a vision where I saw myself in a tornado. I was in the center, seeing things that I had no control over and could not stop. I looked straight first and then noticed that I started going in a circle within the center. I was focusing on everything that was going on and trying to keep it from getting destroyed. I was starting to let the tornado overwhelm me.

After the vision, I realized I was allowing the tornado to distract me. My revelation was the storm had consumed me, and I needed to stop going in circles. (I knew it was a God moment because right after, one of my daughters came into my room and asked to pray for me)

So today, my question is, "Do you realize that you were in the eye of the storm? Have trials and tribulations become, and you are just focusing on perseverance? Or things were building and moving with momentum, and you noticed that distractions started coming, and found yourself focusing more on those situations.

_____

_____

_____

_____

_____

_____

_____

_____

_____

_____

_____

_____

_____

_____

_____

We are faith believers, and sometimes, we forget that Jesus gave us the authority of the storm. Sometimes, we must be reminded.

Mark 4:35-41

35 That day when evening came, he said to his disciples, "Let us go over to the other side." 36 Leaving the crowd behind, they took him along, just as he was, in the boat. There were also other boats with him. 37 A furious squall came up, and the waves broke over the boat so that it was nearly swamped. 38 Jesus was in the stern, sleeping on a cushion. The disciples woke him and said to him, "Teacher, don't you care if we drown?"39 He got up, rebuked the wind, and said to the waves, "Quiet! Be still!" Then the wind died down and it was completely calm.40 He said to his disciples, "Why are you so afraid? Do you still have no faith?"41 They were terrified and asked each other, "Who is this? Even the wind and the waves obey him!" NIV

Matthew 8:23-27

Then Jesus got into the boat and started across the lake with his disciples. 24 Suddenly, a fierce storm struck the lake, with waves breaking into the boat. But Jesus was sleeping. 25 The disciples went and woke him up, shouting, "Lord, save us! We're going to drown!"26 Jesus responded, "Why are you afraid? You have so little faith!" Then he got up and rebuked the wind and waves, and suddenly there was a great calm. 27 The disciples were amazed. "Who is this man?" they asked. "Even the winds and waves obey him!" NLT

The eye of the storm can come through our life challenges, but we must know that we are equipped, that we are firmly standing while Jesus is with us, and that He has given us the authority to say, "Peace Be Still."

Please know your faith is being built, which is part of the process. He will always be there.

Reference Scriptures

Romans 8:18

Yet what we suffer now is nothing compared to the glory he will reveal to us later. KJV

2 Corinthians 12:9

⁹ And he said unto me, My grace is sufficient for thee: for my strength is made perfect in weakness. Most gladly therefore will I rather glory in my infirmities, that the power of Christ may rest upon me. KLV

Psalm 145:18

The LORD is close to all who call on him, yes, to all who call on him in truth. NLT

Hebrews 10:36

Patient endurance is what you need now, so that you will continue to do God's will. Then you will receive all that he has promised. Please be encouraged today and know that the Lord hears your cry(voice). Cry out to him. Seek his face. He collects your tears; Jesus will be with you in the eye of the storm. NLT

Psalm 116:1

I love the LORD because he hears my voice. and my prayer for mercy. NLT

Romans 12:12

Rejoice in our confident hope. Be patient in trouble and Keep on praying. KJV

Romans 8:28

And we know that God causes everything to work together[a] for the good of those who love God and are called according to his purpose for them. KJV

(Feel free to write down some of your thoughts and concerns.)

Preserve and Pray is the key, even in the eye of the storm. The Lord is there. He will calm the storm, and when the storm is over, you will come out stronger because we are overcomers.

Ephesians 6:10-18

[10] Finally, my brethren, be strong in the Lord, and in the power of his might. [11] Put on the whole armour of God, that ye may be able to stand against the wiles of the devil. [12] For we wrestle not against flesh and blood, but against principalities, against powers, against the rulers of the darkness of this world, against spiritual wickedness in high places. [13] Wherefore take unto you the whole armour of God, that ye may be able to withstand in the evil day, and having done all, to stand. [14] Stand therefore, having your loins girt about with truth, and having on the breastplate of righteousness; [15] And your feet shod with the preparation of the gospel of peace; [16] Above all, taking the shield of faith, wherewith ye shall be able to quench all the fiery darts of the wicked. [17] And take the helmet of salvation, and the sword of the Spirit, which is the word of God: [18] Praying always with all prayer and supplication in the Spirit, and watching thereunto with all perseverance and supplication for all saints; KJV

Reflection Moment: Your Uncomfortable Season

Preparing for this message, I had a challenging time trying to name it. I went through three titles and could not produce a comfortable name for the message. That message was so close to what I was going through that I had no words to express or describe (summary). I began to research some scriptures and came across something on Google. So, I give all credit to the title I will present. "Getting Comfortable with the Uncomfortable." This title resonated with me. I agree that I got my revelation of this season when I cried out to God as seasons have changed. This year was quite different from the many other seasons that I had been in. I believe in seasons, and the word even mentions the importance of seasons. This year, I was ready for growth. I was well equipped for what was to come but had no idea it would be so uncomfortable in these past two seasons.

Trials and tribulations are part of life. Throughout the Bible, there have been examples of people of God who have dealt with many situations that challenge their faith. Their livelihood, but I understood pressing in Faith. I understood that the Lord would never put more on us than we could bear.

I envisioned myself jumping out of a plane with my parachute, and my confidence was indeed an expression of "free fall." I knew that the Lord would catch me if I fell; as a matter of fact, I knew he wouldn't let me fall. No, I see myself standing in front of a hot coal line without passing to the other side besides walking across it. I have been walking on my tiptoes trying to make it over, and many times, the heat is so unbearable that I am in pain and tears trying to make it across the hot coals. But I am confident that I will reach the goal. (that is the faith part).

Here are some key points to this passage to encourage you.

There is no Growth without Uncomfortable.

Many of you went from your free-fall walk in life to walking across the hot coals. Do not think it strange. In the heat of it all, in the uncomfortable moments, you have elevated. The altitude is at an on-time high. The Lord has granted you access to another level. In the next level, there is fullness; there are promises. Crushing is the way of preservation for the olive. It's also the way to get what's most valuable, the oil, out of the olive. Keeping this perspective is how we can be troubled on every side yet not distressed ... pressed to the point of being crushed but not crushed and destroyed

James 1

²My brethren, count it all joy when ye fall into divers temptations;³Knowing this, that the trying of your faith worketh patience.⁴But let patience have her perfect work, that ye may be perfect and entire, wanting nothing.⁵If any of you lack wisdom, let him ask of God, that giveth to all men liberally, and upbraideth not; and it shall be given him.⁶But let him ask in faith, nothing wavering. For he that wavereth is like a wave of the sea driven with the wind and tossed.

I had to stop thinking about how uncomfortable it was and ask myself why. You have dealt with the worst. I went through my moments of kicking and screaming. I went through my moment of questioning if I am your servant, and I even went through the leave me alone moment. But I could not stay in them too long. So, I am challenging you not to be in these moments for exceptionally long. The father hears you complain. He collects your tears. He wants to see his perfect will for you. Once again, you may not know it, but you have grown up spiritually. These moments are not going to be always

. _Reference Scriptures_

2 Corinthians 4:8-9

[8] We are troubled on every side, yet not distressed; we are perplexed, but not in despair;[9] Persecuted, but not forsaken; cast down, but not destroyed; KJV

1 Peter 5:7
casting all your care upon Him, for He cares for you. KJV
Psalm 30:5

For His anger is but for a moment,His favor is for life;Weeping may endure for a night,But [a]joy comes in the morning. NLT

Psalm 27:14
Wait on the Lord: be of good courage, and he shall strengthen thine heart: wait, I say, on the Lord. KJV

Isaiah 40:31
But they that wait upon the Lord shall renew their strength; they shall mount up with wings as eagles; they shall run, and not be weary; and they shall walk, and not faint. KJV

1 Peter 1:7
That the trial of your faith, being much more precious than of gold that perisheth, though it is tried with fire, might be found unto praise and honor and glory at the appearing of Jesus Christ: KJV
1 Peter 4:12
Beloved, think it not strange concerning the fiery trial which is to try you, as though some strange thing happened unto you: KJV

Exodus 33:14
And he said, My presence shall go with thee, and I will give thee rest.

Psalm 61:1-2
Hear my cry, O God; attend unto my prayer.[2] From the end of the earth will I cry unto thee, when my heart is overwhelmed: lead me to the rock that is higher than I.KJV

Matthew 11:28-30

28 Come unto me, all ye that labour and are heavy laden, and I will give you rest.29 Take my yoke upon you, and learn of me; for I am meek and lowly in heart: and ye shall find rest unto your souls.30 For my yoke is easy, and my burden is light.KJV

Isaiah 26:3-4

3 Thou wilt keep him in perfect peace, whose mind is stayed on thee: because he trusteth in thee.4 Trust ye in the LORD for ever: for in the LORD JEHOVAH is everlasting strength: KJV

Psalm 94:19

19 In the multitude of my thoughts within me thy comforts delight my soul.

Psalms 119:24

24 Thy testimonies also are my delight and my counselors.

Chapter 9: Jesus Said.

As we navigate to the conclusion of this volume, I want to bring some revelation of how important faith is to your lifestyle in Christ. Coming into your walk with Christ was an act of Faith. Faith is a core principle in our life with Christ. You have walked through types of Faith, the importance of Faith, and the application of Faith. Give yourself some grace. Faith is an eternal principle because our Father is Faith. We thrive in him because he is faithful to his people. He is loyal to you, and he desires that you have everything you need to be a great representation of his kingdom. Our faith is built on a solid foundation. Jesus is his name. As you grow in our God, your faith will reach higher heights.

Our Father, the Savior, brought clarity through the Word when he spoke to Peter. Perseverance is the element that was bought at a price. Through our Savior, Faith is gained. Remember, faith is through and from eternity in life in Christ Jesus. Jesus desires that you evolve into the kingship or queenship you inherited coming into the body of Christ. Faith is continually progressing in life. As you grow in Christ, your Faith will grow, too. Something that Jesus Christ said to Peter was so profound, and I would like to challenge you to gain an understanding of how important Faith is.

In Luke 22:31-32,

Simon, Simon, Satan has asked to sift each of you like wheat. 32 But I have pleaded in prayer for you, Simon, that your faith should not fail. So when you have repented and turned to me again, strengthen your brothers."KJV

Jesus Christ himself went into intercession for the disciple Peter. Jesus let him know that one thing that can remain is your faith; our challenge is not to allow the world and our situations to drag us to fail in our faith in Jesus Christ. The Lord's prayer is when we have moments of doubt, we repent and turn to him. Hallelujah!!! Turn to Jesus!!! There will be testing in our faith and moments of struggle, but we declare that you hold firm to your Faith in the name of Jesus, AMEN.

Hebrews 11:1

"Now faith is confidence in what we hope for and assurance about what we do not see." KJV